SACRED THOUGHT

Sacred Thought

MI'KMAQ MEDITATIONS FOR OUR TIMES

ELDER GEORGE PAUL

POWNAL STREET PRESS
CHARLOTTETOWN

www.pownalstreetpress.com

Pownal Street Press is an independent press that broadens the publishing landscape with a diverse collection of non-fiction and children's picture books.

Sacred Thought: Mi'kmaq Meditations for Our Times
ISBN: 9781998129256 (softcover)
ISBN: 9781998129324 (e-book)

 Edited by Mo Duffy. Proofread by Kate Kennedy. Typeset by Jordan Beaulieu. The text was set in Baskerville.

Pownal Street Press gratefully acknowledges Mi'kma'ki, the ancestral and unceded territory of the Mi'kmaq First Nation on whose land our office is located.

Printed and bound in Canada by Friesens.

1 2 3 4 5 24 25 26 27 28

DEDICATION

I WOULD LIKE TO DEDICATE this project to, first of all, the future generations in my family and all those who were involved in the journey that has been laid before me since the spirits started guiding me towards a better understanding of how to practice traditional ceremonies and prayers. The main person who was very instrumental for all of us here on the East Coast was a man from Hobbema, Alberta, by the name of Albert Lightning a.k.a. "Buffalo Child." Albert Lightning shared with us his life experiences and his encounters with spirits that would communicate to him things to come or what must be done to undo wrongs that were committed to the living or the dead. He taught us how spirits can see what you are thinking and how we must always respect sacred spaces. What offerings to bring for ceremonies and how to conduct ourselves during ceremonies. (Not all ceremonies are the same and may require certain procedures, depending on the nature of the ceremony requested.)

During my journey up until the present day I have met many elders from several nations. I sat and spoke with Mi'kmaq,

Wolastoqey and the Wabanaki family of elders of the East Coast. So many elders and knowledge keepers from Turtle Island and from coast to coast. All the elders and teachers that I participated in ceremonies with, like pipe ceremonies, sweat lodges, Cree Sundance, Lakota Yuwipi ceremony, shaking tent, Medewiwin lodge, Haudenosaunees longhouse at Oka naming ceremonies, Feast for the Departed souls and fasting ceremonies.

If not for their teachings and guidance I would not be where I am today. All those that are dedicated to preserving traditional knowledge and the sacred teachings.

KEPMITE'TAQNEY KTAPEKIAQN

Kepmite'tmnej ta'n teli l'nuwulti'kw
Ni'kma'jtut mawita'nej
Kepmite'tmnej ta'n wetapeksulti'k
Ni'kma'jtut apoqnmatultinej
Apoqnmatultinej ta'n
Kisu'lkw teli ika'luksi'kw ula wksitqamu

Way oh hay hi ya
Ya way yo hay yo hay hi ya
Way yo hay hi ya
Ya way yo hay hi ya
Way yo hay hi ya
way yo hay hi ya
Ya way yo hay ha ya hay yo

CONTENTS

INTRODUCTION

THE "SACRED THOUGHT" IS A CONCEPT of interpreting the life cycle and spiritual teachings of an Indigenous way of life. Since time immemorial this philosophy has been practiced and maintained mainly by the North American Indian tribes. Although several other Indigenous groups around the world have similar understandings, it is the North American First Nations people that are the first people of this continent who have maintained this spiritual practice to the present day. This symbolism applies to a very simple method of understanding life as all Indigenous people do. They don't walk around with a written book of this knowledge; it is more like an everyday experience of life as it unfolds throughout all of their lives. Through lessons learned at different age levels and life experiences, these teachings were handed down from one generation to the next through the oral traditions maintained by the elders of each Indigenous nation. They inhabited the entire continent known to us as Turtle Island, and what has commonly been termed by modern explorers arriving on these shores as the *New World.* Today it's simply North and South America.

Since the dawn of time, Native American tribes and aboriginal groups around the world have practiced this very holistic way of thinking, which continues to this day. Although the spiritual values remain basically the same of human experiences found in their interpretation of this holistic philosophy, the only variance to be found is clearly identified by the type of environment or the geographical location of the people.

More recently, these sacred ways of the Indigenous "Red Man" have opened the eyes of many modern enthusiasts of traditional knowledge on a quest for a better understanding of themselves and the search for the original true meaning of spirituality. These lost souls of our modern times have been searching because over time they have lost their foundation, which is crucial for balance and peace of mind, disconnected from Mother Nature, sometimes feeling trapped within the great confusion of the fast pace of technology and the industrialization that governs the world economy of today.

Although our ancient ancestors may not have developed a writing system put into book form, a lot of what was taught was through oral traditions and the use of symbols relating to our environment and our universe. Each symbol told a story and had a profound impact on those who knew what it meant. These symbols would then be incorporated in the designs they would carve, paint, or weave into everything they used as part of everyday life, especially their ceremonial and sacred objects.

IDENTITY QUEST

TO GET A BETTER PERSPECTIVE ON this philosophy, let's start from square one. Man has always asked such questions as *Who am I?* and *Where do I come from?*, derivatives which pose a challenge to every living, thinking individual who is born into our physical world. When our life clock begins to tick, we also begin to think, and it is this inquisitive nature that drives an insatiable hunger within us to investigate. So the search begins, and off we go on an endless journey to quench our thirst for knowledge. As we embark on the voyage, we explore our environment and how we fit into it. From the tiniest microscopic organisms to the largest living creatures, this drive to seek out all that life can offer applies to all physical living creatures of our world.

WHO AM I?

The first question comes to light when we realize just how much movement we have as living organisms, and when we begin to examine just what the life force is that keeps us propelling forward. It is when we begin to move that we begin to venture beyond our starting points to try and understand how we each relate to the environment.

From the beginning of time, we have known that each of us has a starting point. Even though this may encourage more questions than we anticipated, we might as well go all the way back to the beginning of creation. Since no one knows exactly when that was, let's just say, for now, it was "in the beginning of time." This opens the door to our next question.

WHERE DO I COME FROM?

To exist, we must be an entity, and to be an entity we must be able to reflect or cast a shadow. From our seeds, we begin to grow.

Like all living organisms that have matter, all substantial living organisms contain the building blocks of life known as deoxyribonucleic acid. Without this DNA, it would not be possible to sustain life. This explains the physical nature of our existence. Life in any form must generate some sense of activity, internally or externally, and no doubt rely on some vital source of energy to survive and unfold. It is important to note that this is where the possibilities of intellectual divine thinking may play a vital role in our understanding of how life begins for all living things. Therefore, we can conclude that the beginning of all existence in our universe began with the Big Bang, and that the impetus behind the Big Bang was a thought.

Is it possible . . . that a thought was so powerful and so alive that it manifested and exploded into being? We—the Mi'kmaq—believe that yes, it's the almighty spiritual power of the initiator, projected through his thought beyond infinity. But most importantly, we believe that all living creatures, especially the human family inhabiting our Mother Earth, will come to believe in the higher power referred to as our Great Grandfather Creator, or the Ultimate Deity commonly referred to as God, the great unseen force that is in everything around us.

This unseen force, often referred to as Almighty Power, is organized and governed by its own unique set of laws. First, the physical laws of nature which are fixed and set by its own chemistry, and second, the spiritual laws which link us all to the Great Spirit and the beginning of time itself. The spiritual and the physical intertwine with everything that has been created in this universe. So, everything we experience, and all our actions, cast a shadow. This shadow that I am referring to is our spirit which reflects us out into the spirit world.

The Great Grandfather Creator allows humankind to express free will and to make decisions based on the knowledge of what the consequences may be, of right or wrong, as deemed important by the spiritual guidance that he or she may go through here on Mother Earth. These decisions are stored in our spirit's memory until it is time for us to enter the spirit world, at which time the Great Spiritual Council and Our Great Grandfather Creator welcome us into the spiritual domain.

Morals and teachings of man's spiritual values are handed down through generations of divine teachings and have become the basis of our laws during our physical existence here on the physical plane. All that is acceptable in the eyes of the Creator moves with great passion and emotional fortitude towards life and creativity, and helps encourage positive lifestyles, such as good health, caring, love, and genuine happiness to be alive. All that is negative does the opposite, meaning that it takes away from the good life of all, causing sickness, misery, death, and destruction, leaving a trail of sorrow in its wake. Both these positive and negative energies are part of our everyday living experience, including the mistakes we make, that we may learn from and use as spiritual food to achieve our goals in the future, towards mental, physical, emotional, and ultimately spiritual harmony.

[1]

THE STORY AWAKENING

BEFORE THERE WAS ANYTHING, there was nothing. With nothing to be known and nothing to be seen, this darkness emptied into an endless infinity. And out of this void and perpetuity begins the most beautiful story that will ever be

[1] The Wabanaki symbol.

told, for all time. And so, we begin. Everyone has their own creation story, and this one is mine.

In the beginning of time, when the Great Grandfather Creator, *Gisu'lk Ikji-niskam* (which is how we would say it in our Mi'kmaq language), initiated the thoughts of existence, there was a movement. At that very moment in time and space, there was an almighty explosion that sent vibrations riveting throughout space and subsequently throughout time. This powerful initiate of force created the great thought, and this Big Bang became an awakening. The Great Grandfather Creator's thoughts were of life within an incredibly special universe, a universe that is designed to reflect all his imagination in both the physical and the spiritual realm. These two entities—along with positive and negative energies—began to collide with each other at ultimate high speeds, which is why the event became known as "the awakening."

But for the Great Creator, it wasn't enough. He had to understand what this big bang was, and where it came from. He ordered the stars to shine brightly in their darkness, and to reveal all that is in *Wa'so'qa'si* or the heavens. In doing so, the vibrations of this sound reverberated from the beginning of his thought. He found at first that the vibrations came in groups of four waves.

Then, from within the sound, a spirit spoke. "I am the noise you hear, I am the explosion, and I was born of your great thought. For every action, there is a reaction, therefore I will be the link between the physical and the spiritual. I will be the resounding rhythm and flow of every life form that you create."

"I am the spirit of movement and sound," the Creator continued, "and I will become the rhythm of life and the first Drum—*Pepgwejeda'q.*" And he was happy. But there was more.

"I want to carry every noise and expression that happens within your great creation. Because I was born in thought, I will record everything into memory, so that all that lives in the physical and spiritual realm can be remembered."

And with that, the Creator gave us peace, and a gratitude in our hearts. "I want to be in the hearts and minds of all that sing to you in praise, for the very special gift that you bestow on all the beings and existing in the wonders and joys of life itself." To this, the Great Grandfather Creator said, "*Na Tliaj*—It will be."

WE ARE ALL IN RHYTHM

RHYTHM IS OUR NATURAL INHERITANCE.
It exists in our bodies, our hearts, and our breath.
It exists in the vibration of atoms, the cycles of the seasons,
the ticking of clocks, the orbit of the earth.
There is no part of creation that is without rhythm
or vibration.
It transcends physically and spiritually
from the beginning of time
to infinity.

THE UNIVERSE UNFOLDS

THEN, FROM ANOTHER EXPLOSION that lit up the heavens like fireworks, light spread throughout the darkness to form all of the stars throughout the galaxies of many universes. With all the most beautiful colours imaginable spreading throughout the sea of dark, a tiny portion of this stardust sprinkled down on a newly formed solar system, on the third planet from the sun, which caused it to shine the brightest blue.

At that moment, the Great Grandfather Creator saw this, and designated it to be the dawn of a new era of creation. Therefore, it will become known to all that exist upon it as their mother, our Planet Earth, or *Uksitqamu,* and all life forms above the Earth and below the sea, including all that is beyond, including the solar system, will be its family. Soon after, this became the basis of the spiritual understanding of the six worlds of Mi'kmaq Legends, where nothing happens without a reason, and all creation intertwines with the spiritual. In the chemistry in these explosions there is a meaning so powerful that while it has the capacity to destroy anything in its path, it also has the power to inadvertently create a unique, purposeful life in a microcosm.

Then all of the life spirits that would become part of Mother Earth, be it life upon, above or beneath her, came forward and presented themselves in their own manner. Each held in the palms of their hands their own special ability to apply their co-existence towards peace with every other form of life. To perpetuate life, it was determined that from the tiniest microscopic organism to the most gigantic of creatures, every living thing would have a purpose, and would constantly evolve to fit into their environment. Time has now been set casting its shadow into the spirit world like a duplicate of all our conscious and subconscious destinies manifested through our dreams and visions onto a spiritual memory bank that we can measure with all existing life spans.

GRANDFATHER SUN, GRANDMOTHER MOON, AND FIRE SPIRIT

TIME WILL BE GOVERNED by a symbol of the Great Grandfather Creator's power, and will provide light and energy to the rest of the solar system. This will be known as *Niskaminu Na'gu'set,* or the Sun Spirit, and will be referred to as Grandfather Sun within our universal family. With the awakening of every new day, Grandfather Sun will be a constant reminder of the Great Grandfather Creator's thoughts and his master plan. The Sun Spirit offers the gift of fire; this is one of four sacred elements that are vital to all existing life forms upon Mother Earth. Grandfather Sun assists Grandmother Moon, *Nugumi,* at night by giving her the light to reflect down onto her grandchildren whether it be bird, fish, plant, insect, animal or humans, to help them stimulate their growth hormones and fertility.

She is high enough to orbit around Mother Earth's space to reach the light from Grandfather Sun, and that is why in Mi'kmaq we call her *Tepgunaset.*

These powerful forces would devastate the delicate balance of Mother Earth if it were not for Father Sky, *Musigisk*, who protects Mother Earth by giving her a special magnetic field to deflect solar flares with a shield called atmosphere. This philosophical protective family trait is mirrored down and would apply to all families of our world with their own form of shields and protection to survive.

Fire spirit holds a concentrated energy so powerful that the heat generated within its core could melt or even disintegrate any physical form. All humankind has been given the privilege to use this sacred fire, *Ekjibuktew*, but with caution. There is a real danger that if humankind abuses this special gift, by way of nuclear bombs and weapons, he may wind up destroying his own world and all that lives upon it. We are all subjected to the powers of these elements and need to know how to understand and balance the four basic building blocks of life very carefully.

THE FOUR ELEMENTS

NOTHING EXISTS IN ISOLATION; everything exists only relative to something else. The four elements remind us of this. In Mi'kmaq, these four elements are called *Maqamigew* (Earth), *Buktew* (Fire), *Samqwan* (Water), and *Ukju'sn* (Air) and they are more than the sum of their parts. These components are vital for life to exist and flourish upon Mother Earth, and they exist in all creatures, whether it is plant, animal, bird, or fish.

Physical, mental, spiritual: we see these not only in our everyday activities, but also through the things we do to stay alive, be it our need for sustenance, for breath, to replenish our fluids, and most importantly, to feed the fire within us, which is our life's electrical energy.

Since the dawn of time, humankind has been developing highly intellectual and sophisticated lifestyles to fit its environments. The way that humankind has realized to harness the energy from the four sacred elements to benefit from the potential of its mighty powers, has been nothing short of miraculous.

INTRODUCTION TO THE SACRED WHEEL

WITH BALANCE COMES CLARITY. Empty the mind, then focus on being in harmony with your soul. The universe and our world within it will continue to exist and do what it naturally does; you have to find that balance within yourself to attain the peace and harmony you need for your own spiritual enlightenment. Apologies in advance for sounding like a guru.

The original medicine wheels, some of which are over five thousand years old, were stone structures built to represent ancient Sacred Wheels. The oldest that we know of was discovered in old Majorville Cairn, in southern Alberta, Canada. There is evidence of dancing and ceremonies on some of these Sacred Wheel sites.

Depending on what part of Turtle Island you are on, the Sacred Wheel (also known as the Medicine Wheel) brings with it some slight differences in the philosophies, while certain meanings remain similar.

The Medicine Wheel is unique; it does not originally exist anywhere else in the world, nor does it represent races, as some believe in error. The Sacred Wheel of today has been redefined and distorted to suggesting each colour represents a race, yet when the original wheels were built, Native people had no contact with any other races. This inclusive symbolism signifies a spiritual awakening; it is a new era of understanding.

The Sacred Wheel represents the four corners of our land, with the following colours representing seasons as they change direction. The East white quadrant represents morning, spring, and birth. The South yellow quadrant represents midday, summer, and adulthood. The West red quadrant represents evening, fall, and the elder phase of life. The North black quadrant represents night, winter, being a senior, and death.

As Native Aboriginals, it is imperative that we reclaim *our culture* and what is ancient and sacred within it. For too long, we have adapted our ways to accommodate the ways of others, and we must discontinue this. Others may participate in our sacred ceremonies, but must not try to conduct them on their own, or claim that they have earned the rite. Language is the key to our sacred ceremonies, to communicate with our ancestors, and they respond in the ancient language. Only in this way will our spirituality continue to be respected. *Tahoe!*

GREAT-GRAN

FAT

GRANDMOTHER MOON

M

SPIRIT GUIDE: POLAR BEAR

COLOUR: BLACK

SEASON: WINTER, COLD-ICE-SNOW

PHYSICAL

SPIRIT GUIDE: BEAR, GOOD MEDICINE

COLOUR: RED, BLOOD SEASON

SEASON: FALL, AUTUMN, HUNTING

SACRED MEDICINE: CEDAR

ELEMENT: FIRE

RELATIONSHIPS - ELDERS - TEACHERS - ADVICE

WISDOM - STRENGTH - MALE GENDER

EM

SPIRIT GUIDE: THUNDER BEINGS, BIRDS

COLOUR: YELLOW

SEASON: SUMMER

HER CREATOR
SKY

GRANDFATHER SUN

L

SACRED MEDICINE: OYSTER FUNGUS

ELEMENT: AIR

SENIOR - DEATH - FOCUS - ANCESTORS

E 0

SPIRITUAL

SPIRIT GUIDE: EAGLE

COLOUR: WHITE, PURITY, INNOCENCE

SEASON: SPRING, BIRTH, AWAKENING

SACRED MEDICINE: SWEETGRASS

ELEMENT: WATER, YOUTH

TIME - LIGHT - ENERGY - WARMTH

NAL

SACRED MEDICINE: BUFFALO SAGE

ELEMENT: MOTHER EARTH

GROWTH - ADULT - SOCIAL ACTIVITIES

FEMALE GENDER - LOVE

THE TEACHINGS

THE TEACHINGS OF THE SACRED WHEEL, or *Sabe'wig Guto'qa'taqan,* basically incorporate the most significant or dominant influences of life forms, and are very similar from tribe to tribe, although the fundamentals of everyday life would be particular to those natural environments that each Native American tribe co-exists with.

To interpret the philosophy of spiritual understanding, all life forms such as the birds, fish, plants and animals must be taken into consideration and added into the equation. The movement of spiritual forces, be they positive or negative on all life, no matter how minute, have vast reverberations on the planet and on our being.

Some may say that since humankind has knowledge of how these forces can assist us in the success of our lives, attributed of course to our invention and the use of our technology, that we have accomplished significant achievements. And in a way, this is true. However, it is with humble insights that we must remain vigilant in our beliefs. With our insights of this kind of spiritual intellect, we must be cautious yet disciplined to give way to this understanding of spiritual values and teach all those who seek to understand balance and power. This is understood to be a contract between the divine connection of the Great Creator and man.

Take the use of introducing a foreign species into an unknown environment. Even though we have come a long way from Rachel Carson's *Silent Spring*, it is best practice and common understanding to use what is obvious and relevant around you, rather than to try and interpret something of an unknown origin or something that is not common to our world of understanding. When a foreign species is introduced to a new environment, like a bird, fish, plant, or animal, something that does not logically belong there, oftentimes it creates disruption in the already present ecosystem. We all have our limitations to be able to adapt.

So, the commonsense approach has become an integral part of everyday life in decision making and moving forward with plans or activities regarding our well-being. Furthermore, common sense thinking almost always follows the laws of nature, to which we concur that Natural Law has precedence over the flow of the physical life here on Mother Earth. All of this philosophy is broken down into four components in the Sacred Wheel teachings, each component having its own set of physical and spiritual laws.

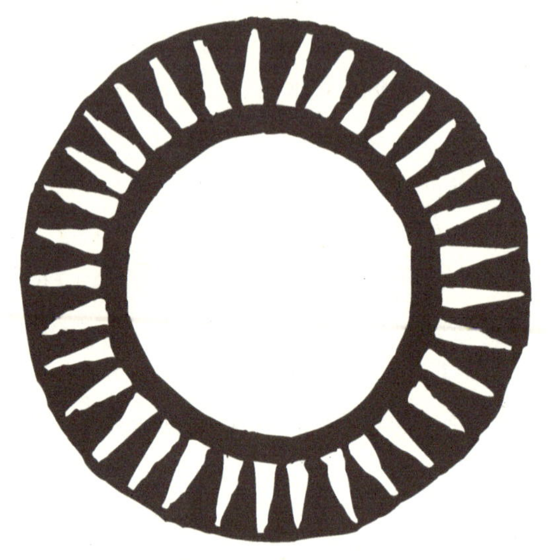

EAST

DIRECTION = EAST

SEASON = SPRING

SPIRIT GUIDE = EAGLE

ELEMENT = WATER

COLOUR = WHITE

STAGE OF LIFE = BIRTH/CHILDHOOD

MEDICINE = SWEETGRASS

ATTRIBUTE = SPIRITUALITY

GIFT = INNOCENCE/FAITH

The first position on the Sacred Wheel is East. This is the common-sense approach. There are many other interpretations of the four colours and how they are placed in the wheel, but the common-sense approach uses the diagram with the colours gradually getting darker as they progress moving clockwise depicting stages of growth and aging, moving from white to yellow to red to black to represent the beginning to the end of a life cycle.

Sometimes I like to explain the four sacred colours this way: When I was a child growing up on the reservation I used to watch my mom cooking homemade bread. I watched the process from start to finish. When she first put the bread in the oven it was all white, and as I watched it cooking it started to rise and turn yellow because of being in a heated oven. The longer it was in the heat the darker it got and began to turn a reddish hue indicating it was cooked. If it stayed in the oven for too long it got burnt and turned black. It's the simplest explanation I can give about the process of life.

To fully understand the Sacred Wheel, one must live it.

To the East where the sun rises, we get our first light. This energy is so full, we can only compare it with being born. At the very moment of birth, we are exposed to all the elements and the influences of Mother Earth and the Universe.

This is an immensely powerful and symbolic transition for coming into the light. From our mother's womb as children, we are born with a new spirit, one that is pure, innocent and devoid of any negative or evil influence. The dawn of spirituality makes its entrance from the East, and so we look towards the East for spiritual understanding and enlightenment.

When light exposes us all from the darkness, we can see both physically and spiritually. With all that is revealed before us, we become comfortable to move forward because the fear of the unknown is no longer a factor. With each new day, we welcome the knowledge of the spiritual teachings from our Great Creator with unconditional love. This trait can be seen in all the children of the world, through their quickness to forgive.[2] The spiritually pure, clean, and innocent can only be represented by the colour white. Therefore, the colour white is placed in the East symbolizing, light, purity, innocence, and spirituality. These new beginnings can take place within us at any and all ages.

In the spring of the year, like when a woman's water breaks before a child is born, the winter ice melts and flows out to the sea. Without the sacred element of water, in the building blocks of life, nothing can grow or live. Water thus becomes of ultimate importance.

When seeds open to bloom, timed with all earthly life forms awakening from hibernation, they begin their spiritual

[2] Read more about this in my last chapter, "A Song to Awaken the Spirit."

life cycle. Instinctively, this repeats every year. Birds build their nests and lay their eggs. Insects prepare to pollinate plants and churn the soil to be fertile, fish swim up rivers and streams to spawn, and animals give birth to their young. Everywhere, sweet-scented flowers display beautiful colours pleasing to the eye, and the world becomes just like the rainbow against the clear blue sky.

To the East, we are given the gift to be able to communicate with the spiritual world. But to exercise spirituality we must obey the divine teachings. Through intermediaries, the Great Creator hands down to us these teachings that we affectionately call spirit guides.

The most significant in this direction of course is Grandfather Sun, or *Niskaminu Na'gu'set.* He shares his gift in the form of fires that keep us warm, cure our food, and shape our tools. But closely behind *Niskaminu Na'gu'set* is the bird of vision, or the Eagle Spirit, known to our people as *Gitpu. Gitpu* flies the highest and sees the farthest, protects us and carries our prayers to the spirits above. Through the Eagle Spirit, we are connected to the Great Spirit, and thus, back to the Creator.

UNDERSTANDING SPIRITUALITY

THE EAGLE STEERS US AWAY from anything negative ahead and teaches us to be ever alert for those that may want to do us harm—whether that be physical or spiritual, now or in the future. Legends of the Eagle Spirit handed down for generations are told from tribe to tribe of a time when there were only *N'nu'g* or *Ilnu'g,* the human people existing on this continent. According to our creation stories, the original people of this continent were placed here by the Creator himself, to multiply and flourish into many diverse communities. Every tribe had great spiritual powers granted to them by the Great Creator, including their own language and lifestyle. Incredibly special abilities were bestowed on certain individuals of each tribe who were called *Ginaps* and *Buoins. Ginaps* were born with special gifts of strength and vision, while *Buoins* were more like dreamers, or sorcerers, and the natural spirits drawn from creatures and plants of the environment.

Among the Wabanaki there lives a legend of our own cultural hero, Glooscap, who had to deal with his evil brother, Malsum. Based on the stories that I have heard from Elders and some of the writings of Silas T. Rand, Canadian ethnologist, linguist and translator who was known to record from the Elders one of the earliest profiles of Glooscap, I've pieced together this interpretation to explain the beginning of the world the brothers would create.

GLOOSCAP AND HIS TWIN BROTHER MALSUM

THE WABANAKI CONSISTS OF A group of five tribes in the northeastern part of Turtle Island. They are the Mi'kmaq, Maliseet, Penobscot, Passamaquoddy, and the Abenaki. Among this family of tribes lives a couple of creation stories. I will tell the legend of two demigods that came down from the Spirit World to create a peaceful society where we may live in harmony. As told in this legend, it all started in the Spirit World where spirits are born. Only this time there were tragic circumstances.

At first, there were twins, who were known as Glooscap and Malsum.[3] When Glooscap and Malsum were in their mother's womb, they were vying for position to be born first, in order to retain ultimate power and control. The first brother born was Glooscap, who was born in the natural way, through his mother's birth canal. This enraged his brother Malsum, who vented his frustration by bursting his way through his mother's side and out from under her ribs, which killed her in the process.

Glooscap, who was born first, became responsible for his brother and together they both had to face judgment by the Creator for Malsum's insidious act of aggression. The sentence was severe but just, and was as the Creator wanted it. For their punishment, they were forced to leave the spirit world, and to live upon Mother Earth, surviving by their own wits.

As a punishment, Malsum is asked to follow Glooscap, to learn how to better understand his emotions and behaviours through his own manifestations and creativity. Glooscap, in turn, is asked to watch Malsun, and guide him so that he may

[3] Malsum and Malsun are used interchangeably in the legends, and I have used both here.

overcome his anger and aggressive behaviour. But what Glooscap does not know is that Malsum is hiding more than anger and aggression; he carries also the quality of envy, and is jealous of Glooscap being the natural-born leader. He now intends to outdo him.

Glooscap and Malsum have God-like powers here upon Mother Earth, and can shape shift or create anything at will. It is told that they arrived in a granite stone canoe and landed on a shore of red clay in the northeastern part of Turtle Island, where they set up camp. Glooscap tells Malsum that they should work and live together in one camp. But Malsum decides that he will make his own camp, separate from where Glooscap has decided. In almost no time at all, Glooscap has set up his camp, including finding a sacred site where he will communicate with the Creator every day and report on how things are going.

Glooscap and Malsum are granted the power to create everything that they will need in their environment, including the birds, fish, plants, and animals. As they create each form of life, they impart onto them an element of their spiritual powers and abilities. Glooscap created creatures that lived in harmony with nature, while Malsum created creatures that were vicious and plants that were poisonous. To keep him company, Glooscap created a dog that was pure white and named him *Na'gweg*, which means day. Malsum created a dog also, but his dog was pure black, and he named him *Pegenuk*, which means darkest night.

To create the Mi'kmaq people, Glooscap shot an arrow with his magic bow at a black ash tree, and split it open, thus giving birth to the Mi'kmaq people. Malsum, in turn, created a creature half-man half-animal to do his bidding, and named him Lux. Lux spies on Glooscap, to find out what Glooscap's ultimate weakness might be.

But Lux was not happy with his form, so after spying on Glooscap, who was praying to the Creator, he overheard Glooscap telling the Creator what his only weakness was. Anxious to get back to his master now with this new knowledge, Lux planned to make a deal with Malsum, but this valuable piece of information came with a price. With excitement, Lux demanded that Malsum give him a pair of wings so that he could fly. This infuriated Malsum, and he scolded Lux and threatened that if he did not tell him what he had learned, he would turn him into a frog.

After learning the one thing he always wanted to know about Glooscap, Malsum drove Lux away with an angry tantrum. Guilty of his evil deed, Lux went back to Glooscap to tell him of what he had done, and that Malsum was now preparing to kill him. While Lux even tried the same bargaining trick with Glooscap, the demigod stared him down, and forced him to tell him, to be fair, what Malsun's weakness was.

The stage was now set for Malsun and Glooscap to duel to the death. Using all their powers, the two turned themselves into giants taller than trees. As they stomped the ground, wrestled, and fell, they created rivers and lakes, and pushed up the ground to make the hills, mountains, and valleys that shape the landscape of the Wabanaki people of today.

Glooscap wins the battle, but he doesn't kill his brother. Instead, he turns him to stone along with the two dogs (Day and Night) to guard Malsun until Glooscap returns. "I am sorry, my brother, that we have failed to overcome the evil of violence in your heart," Glooscap said to Malsun. "Now I must leave because our act of war has marked the ground on which we live."

He continued, "It will take time for you to heal, but I will return when the time is right and my people have survived the change that is coming. I will leave some special gifts with my people, spiritual powers that will help them get through difficult times. The only caveat is that they should believe in the power of the Creator and respect all forms of life on Earth."

All the birds, animals, and people begged Glooscap to stay. The loon cried up and down the river with his haunting call, asking Glooscap if he could go with him. Glooscap then called for all the fishes of the ocean to come forward until he saw the whale. He asked the whale if he would take him south, and he said yes, providing that Glooscap gave him a pipe to smoke. And so, Glooscap stood on Whale's back, and while the whale was puffing up a trail of smoke, he swam as far South as he could in the ocean.

From Glooscap, the people learned to live off the land with what they were taught. Some of the people had spiritual powers, could shape-shift to travel underwater or to fly, or had other great strength and able to do fantastic feats. They lived in harmony for an exceptionally long time.

Eventually, there came a time when they started abusing these powers by competing with one another to destroy each other. The Creator took matters into his own hands and decided to punish the people by bringing the sun closer and burning the face of Mother Earth, which would cleanse the evildoers.

But because Eagle had been given the special ability to see into the future, he saw what was going to take place, flew high up towards the sun screaming four times at the Great Grandfather Creator as he flew into the spirit realm, leaving his physical form behind. The Great Grandfather Creator heard the eagle's cry and stated with a thundering voice, "Speak your request!"

Eagle Spirit replied, "Not all the people have gone astray from your original teachings. Observe certain tribes, those who still sit quietly by their campfires, who meditate for the good health and happiness for all their people. Surely this must have the merits to spare the humble and meek from your almighty wrath, Oh Great Creator! Punish those who have committed crimes against the sacred and holy ways that you have gifted but allow me to offer myself to assist those who are sincere and follow your teachings in a sincere sacred manner."

Eagle continued, "I will be their instrument to rid of evil any places that are deemed sacred for ceremonies, this promise I will keep to you." To this the Great Grandfather Creator said, "It shall be."

So, the eagle spirit flew down to Mother Earth and appeared to those who were meditating and fasting on vision quests and told this story to those teachers as they meditated by their sacred fires. "I have offered myself for you to use in your ceremonies and protect what you deem sacred."

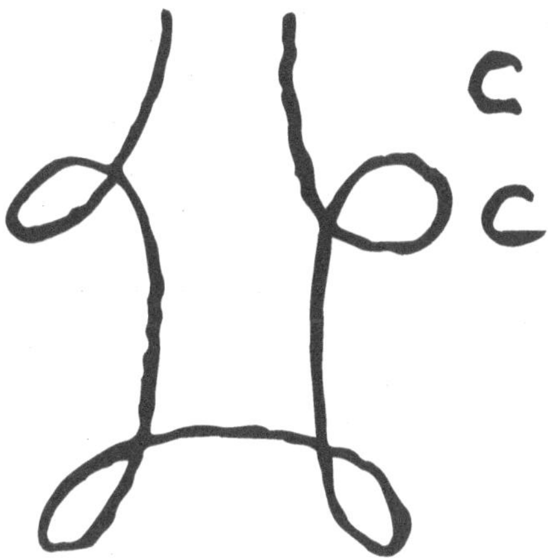

From then on and to this very day, you will see Native American Indigenous people honouring the eagle for its sacrifice. They do this by wearing eagle feathers in their hair and on their regalia when they dance, and keeping feathers in their vehicles when they travel, and when conducting sacred ceremonies, because it protects and restores honour and respect to all people who follow the *Ilnu* sacred spiritual teachings (denoted by the symbol above). Like the eagle, the teachings represent a freedom of spirituality. A culture of living in harmony with nature will intertwine with teachings and values of spiritual understanding throughout Turtle Island, and all Indigenous people will conduct their lives with respect and ceremony.

It is important to respect the process of engaging in ceremony, and these spirit guides must follow procedures and protocol. There are four sacred medicines that are required to open the door of these four directions; to each direction is one specific sacred medicine. Here in the eastern part of the country, it is sweetgrass, sometimes referred to as Mother Earth's hair. One of the sweetest-smelling grasses in the world, this grass is like it has been shampooed and conditioned, leaving it soft, shiny, and flowing. It is one of the most powerful medicines we have, because it is said to open the door to the spiritual realm; it can cleanse us to make us presentable in the eyes of the spiritual council and the Creator that hears our prayers.

For all the special blessings that the Ilnu enjoy in life, prayers are requested and brought forward by the Great Grandfather Creator for approval. Not all prayers are answered, and some are required to be repeated several times before they can be sincere, for only the most humble and sincere prayers are given response. Prayers are like our quiet appeals seeking spiritual assistance, to either guide us towards a happier life, or to bestow upon us good health and well-being.

NOTHING FOR NOTHING: ON OFFERINGS

One discipline that we practice to show good faith of our commitment to our partnership with the spirit world is to place offerings. This is a symbol that nothing is given for nothing. Through our spiritual healers and teachers, we are taught to always pay proper respect at all ceremonies by bringing an offering. Through our communication with the spirits, we know what is necessary for offerings. With the spirits we make these bonds, and we must be careful not to insult them by bringing something else. These teachings are then handed down in a traditional manner from one generation to the next. The first offering has always been known to be tobacco, and then all others may vary per the type of ceremony being conducted. Every movement and gesture you make during the ceremony is observed by the spiritual council in the spirit realm and taken into consideration as part of your authenticity. Ultimately, we pay our utmost respect to the Great Grandfather Creator and the spirit world because that is where we came from in the beginning, and it is the place we will return to in the end.

SOUTH

DIRECTION = SOUTH
SEASON = SUMMER
SPIRIT GUIDE = THUNDER BIRD
ELEMENT = MOTHER EARTH
COLOUR = YELLOW
STAGE OF LIFE = ADULTHOOD
MEDICINE = BUFFALO SAGE
ATTRIBUTES = EMOTIONAL
GIFT = LOVE, FEMALE GENDER

SOUTH IS OFTEN REFERRED TO as the place of warm weather, a place where the elderly like to vacation to, when the winter season hits. Even the birds migrate South towards warmer conditions when the food source is depleted here in the northern regions of Turtle Island, and the wild northwest winds blow. It is a natural passage to return to the North, as soon as the season unfolds the colours of flowers and foliage. It's no wonder that our ancestors believe the true spirit of Mother Earth can be represented with love and growth in this direction, and all the female gender carries the emotional genes from one generation to the next.

The constant flow of the Universe affects us all, as it unfolds the pages of time and space. This movement that we understand to be the universal flow has a direction that coincides with man's invention of the clock, and its direction travels in a circumference from left to right. So, if we are to follow the universal flow and move clockwise starting from East, our next reference point is South. On the clock's face, this would be at high noon. If the clock were to represent the the human life span, we would now be entering adulthood.

In the adult stage of life, we are warm, comfortable. The warmest colour on the colour chart is yellow and is often associated by artists of all ages with the colour of the sun. As we travel from East to South, we learn and grow out of each season and adapt to our life's changes as they develop right before our eyes. It's like a Polaroid picture as it exposes, becoming clearer and clearer by the moment. As the buds open and reveal all the flowers with every colour of the rainbow, the beauty and splendor of life enters yet another stage of growth where all the green foliage of trees and grasses of Mother Earth become full and rich with nutrition for every other living creature, in the process linking the chain of life to all living organisms through their sustenance. The fact that we refer to the Earth as our mother is no surprise, because in the same way our mothers feed us and nurture us as we grow, taking care of all our needs. As creatures of this world, we are very dependent, and we need each other to survive. We must constantly eat and drink and have the proper nutrition.

For instance, when the mayflowers came out our people would pick them to make tea, hair decorations, and perfumes because of their sweet scent. We would celebrate all the berries as they ripened such as strawberries, cherries, blueberries, gooseberries, and cranberries. Nuts, tubers, roots, and a variety of wild vegetables including some leaves and barks would add to the extensive and nutritious diet that is always available within our region. All throughout the summer months our ancestors gathered diverse types of foods and medicines as they became ripe for the picking.

When we look towards the South, we honour the female gender of all life forms and respect their roles as the givers of life. *E'pit,* or the Woman Spirit, teaches us about compassion, caring, sharing, and understanding the emotional balance that we must maintain to live with the proper discipline and cleanliness needed to sustain a healthy communal environment. The cool rains and the warm sun provide ideal conditions for growth. When we are young, it is a time to travel about and explore and enjoy the beauty of nature, ever increasing our knowledge of the organic fertile gifts from the South and the generous outpouring of its summer season.

Among the many types of herbs and plants that we Native Americans use for food and medicines is sage, but there is one herb that is associated with its use for protection, and it is a sacred medicine for this direction: the buffalo sage. The buffalo, *Mestugepegajit,* protect their young by forming a large circle,

then forcing the young and the weak towards the centre, the larger and stronger ones forming an impenetrable wall on the outside. The spirit of this plant is said to have protective powers, protecting us against any evil that will try to disrupt us—like jealousy and greed.

LEGEND OF THE THUNDER BEINGS

WHEN WE LOOK AROUND TO appreciate the life, growth, and energy of this season, it is clearly visible what the term *growth* can mean, and how important it is to be connected to the Almighty Living Forces which make themselves heard loudly and clearly all throughout the summer months. Yes, of course

I am speaking about thunder and the Thunder Beings or *Gaqtugwaq*.

Thunder and lightning combine the forces of the negative and positive energies both above and below us. Lightning is the most powerful source of natural energy, feared by all mortals on Mother Earth. In mythology, the mighty thunderbolt has long been feared in many cultures, a magical atmospheric flash which seems to have supernatural origins: the almighty weapon of the gods. The Greeks, for instance, feared and marvelled at Zeus for his authority to wield at his command the power of lightning. The Vikings saw Thor creating lightning by striking an anvil as he rode across the clouds in his chariot. In the Far East, Buddha was said to have carried a thunderbolt with arrows at each end.

In our territory, we have our own legends around thunder and the Thunder Beings. Some of our Native American brothers believed the lightning was due to the flashing feathers of a powerful mystical bird, known as the Thunder Bird, which the Mi'kmaw refer to as *Gaqtugwaw Sisip* or *Gulu*. Thunder Bird is like the condor, whose flapping wings produced the fierce winds and thunder. It's not until we experience the power and the force of these elements that we learn to appreciate its purpose within this season and the electrifying jolt of life it provides for all living creatures.

We include the Thunder Beings in our prayers, and place

offerings so that we may be blessed with a well-balanced season of rain and sunshine throughout the summer months that fill our needs for a healthy harvest in the fall. It is important to celebrate every harvest, to rejoice in its abundance and to give thanks for its purpose to enhance life and the value of food and medicine

WE ARE ONE

WE HAVE ALWAYS LISTENED TO the wise words of our elders regardless of which tribe or geographical location they are from. The wisdom of our brothers and sisters from the far South is still respected by all people. A good example of this is the prophecy of the Mayan calendar, and its exact calculation of certain prophecies.

Mayan elder, researcher and anthropologist Carlos Barrios of the Ajq'ij (Eagle Clan) explains in his work, *The Book of Destiny*,

> Meditation and spiritual practice are good, but also action. It is very important to be clear about who you are, and about your relation to the Earth. Develop yourself with your own tradition and the call of your heart. But remember to respect differences and strive for unity. Learn some good breathing techniques, so you have mastery of your breath. Be clear. Follow a tradition with great roots. It is not important what

> tradition, your heart will tell you, but it must have great roots . . .
>
> We live in a world of energy. An important task now is to learn to sense or see the energy of everyone and everything, people, plants, and animals. This becomes increasingly important as we draw close to the World of the Fifth Sun, for it is associated with the element 'ether' the realm where energy lives and weaves. Go to the sacred places of the Mother Earth to pray for peace, and have respect for she gives us our food, clothing, and shelter. We need to reactivate the energy of these sacred places. That is our work.

Carlos Barrios reminds us that this is a crucially important moment for humanity, and for the Earth. Each person is important. Be who you are with all your heart and work together as one. The greatest wisdom is in simplicity. Seek love, respect, tolerance, sharing, gratitude, and forgiveness. Find your heart, and you will find your way.

WEST

DIRECTION = WEST

SEASON = FALL

SPIRIT GUIDE = BLACK BEAR

ELEMENT = FIRE

COLOUR = RED

STAGE OF LIFE = ELDER TEACHER

MEDICINE = CEDAR

ATTRIBUTES = PHYSICAL, STRENGTH

GIFT = HUMILITY/COURAGE/MALE GENDER

WEST IS THE POSITION WHERE THE sun sets and is the strongest in growth of all living things. In fact it symbolizes maturity and reaching the pinnacle of a life well lived. Now is the time to share and teach those that are learning from the senior elders more wisdom from generations before. The teachings of life are all about the mental, physical, spiritual, and emotional which makes for good medicine ways. We should not think of ourselves as a human family above all other creatures. We are part of the bigger picture that is not just of our Mother Earth, but the whole universe and all of creation.

As we watch the sun move across the sky throughout the day, it's like watching the times of our lives go by in stages. As the moments pass, we move constantly and change position, aging every second. As we develop, we see ourselves changing as well, as we age into situational roles based on our knowledge and life experiences for that time or moment.

These roles determine a level of respect for the knowledge that elders have acquired, whether throughout their lives, or in their fields of expertise. Younger people may then look up to those that have achieved certain status in life, not only because of their diligence, but because they embody their ideology over the course of time. These elders represent the wisdom and knowledge of how to appreciate a good way of life, and how goals can be achieved through persistence and dedication.

Knowing how to achieve these goals, and the careful

curation of planning, is half the battle, so it is natural to want to seek this guidance from our teachers, the mature adults or other community elders. These community members are the pillars and the foundation of a healthy society. All throughout the history of humankind we learn lessons from countless leaders and great role models who have come before us, and from those who have dedicated their lives for the betterment of human existence around the world. We know this through recordings of documented history in the form of writing, pictograms, symbolism, and numerous rituals, ceremonies, and elaborate forms of dancing, chanting, and songs created since the dawn of civilization.

Unfortunately, though, we haven't always been nations interacting peacefully. To show off our strength as men, and to represent the male gender, we have often taken things into our own hands, using whatever acts of aggression were needed to show off. When these animalistic primal instincts kicked in, it led us through many acts of war. The more organized we were with these acts of aggression, the more powerful we became. Millions of human lives have been lost throughout the ages because of man's hunt for power and control, including a number of mass killings, which were developed to perpetuate war.

What is the real reason for calling on such a devastating act of destruction? we may ask ourselves. *For what purpose and to what end?* Can these acts be justified by the tyranny of dictators?

One of the most hurtful instances that this century has seen of this is the residential school system. Between two warring factions, there is often propaganda, aimed to win the hearts and minds of the people on both sides. In most cases, it is the populations with the best strategies, resources, and funds that win out in the end.

A valuable lesson for us in the history of time has been to look back, and to look closely at our history to see where we've come from, so that we may begin to see where we are going. Learning from mistakes makes us wise. Never miss an opportunity to embrace failure, the wise ones say, as those who don't learn from their mistakes may repeat them. We learn more from our failures than from our successes: it's an old cliché, but it still exists. Understanding the value of life's lessons is our greatest challenge, and these are the pearls of wisdom we sift out when gleaning back through the pages of time.

So naturally, there is a clear connection between this component of the medicine wheel, which focuses on our aging men and women, and wisdom, and the season it represents which is the fall of the year. In fall, all the plant life has reached its maximum peak of growth and is ready to reap or be harvested. It's also a time of year when all the animals that we use for food are fattened for consumption. In ancient times, some of the smaller tribes who were hunters and gatherers would move where the food source was plentiful. This meant following the seasons, to capitalize on what each season or region could provide.

Mother Nature provides foods and medicines in every season; yet it is up to us to seek and find its source. Every tribe had their medicine people and hunters who were specialists in their fields, and both genders were included in these roles. These people, highly regarded by their communities, often were raised with this purpose in mind, being taught their necessary lessons by the elders from childhood. It is a sophisticated training system that is still practiced among many aboriginal tribes to this very day.

An example is our brothers and sisters from the farthest

west of Turtle Island, those who live along the Pacific coast under the tallest red cedar, or modern-day Vancouver Island. Most tribes there use cedar for different occasions, although primarily as medicine; it can ward off negative spirits or bad luck so that it brings them prosperity in health and well-being. Cedar medicine was also used for warding off viruses of colds and flus that were emitted by sweating during a fever. Caution was taken not to use too much of it, if taken internally. All Indigenous people of the Americas know this medicine and it is widely used throughout the world.

A legend amongst the Coast Salish peoples describes the origins of the western red cedar. In this legend, there was a generous man who gave the people whatever they needed. When the Great Spirit saw this, he declared that when the generous man died, a great red cedar tree would grow where he was buried, and that the cedar would be useful to all the people, providing its roots for making baskets, its bark for making clothing, and its wood for making shelter.

But of course, the most famous of all the structures that was ever built of red cedar was and still is the totem pole. The designs on totem poles are considered as sacred and as varied as the cultures that make them. The Mi'kmaq also made smaller marker poles which were much like our West Coast brothers' style and had clan symbols on them of animals, birds, or water creatures, and were called *Wa'ji'j*. Totem poles may recount familiar legends, clan lineages, or even notable events. Some poles celebrate cultural beliefs, but others are mostly artistic presentations.

Certain types of totem poles are part of mortuary structures, and incorporate grave boxes with carved supporting poles, or recessed backs for the grave boxes of ancestors. These upright shafts illustrate stories that commemorate historic persons, represent shamanic powers, or provide objects of public ridicule. The vertical order of images has always been widely believed to be a significant representation of importance. This idea is so pervasive that it has entered common parlance with the phrase, "he's the low man on the totem pole." This phrase is indicative of the most common belief of ordering importance, that the higher figures on the pole are more important or prestigious.

THE SEVEN HUNTERS AND THE BEAR

THERE IS A LEGEND TOLD IN the Mi'kmaq Nation about a time when our people lived in harmony with the universe. It was during the ancient times when everyone lived off nature in the humblest way. Several Mi'kmaq communities were spread across the northeastern portion of Turtle Island and had close ties with their neighbouring tribes called the

Wabanaki. Their given names were drawn from the clan they were born into, and how they connected with the environment and the universe as they perceived it back then. So, their names would be of birds, fish, animals, or plant life.

The story of the seven hunters, *Netuulite'wk*, is a prime example of how the ancient Mi'kmaq understood the intertwining connection with the physical and spiritual universe. The big dipper would represent the "Great Bear," Ursa Major. The three stars of the handle of the dipper, or the tail of the bear, they say are the first three of the seven hunters who pursue the bear across the northern sky during the warm summer months: Robin (because it is a reddish star), Chickadee (because it is small like a chickadee), and Moose Bird (Grey Jay). In the constellation Boötes are the other four hunters who lose the chase as they drop from sight below the northern horizon in the late summer: Pigeon, Blue Jay (because it is a blue star), Owl *(Ku'gu'gwesu)*, and the *Saw-whet* (the barn owl).

Our story begins with one of the seven Mi'kmaq hunters named *Jugwi'ges*, Chickadee, and like the chickadee he is small in stature and always moving about quickly. He likes to chat a lot, sometimes even to himself. You might know somebody like that in your community. In fact, all of the characters in this story you may find familiar because as a human family, our behaviour is very similar no matter where we're from.

Picture an ancient scenario on Turtle Island: A beautiful

pristine forest surrounds a traditional Mi'kmaq community near a peaceful flowing river. *Jugwi'ges* is out on a stroll just outside the village late one spring afternoon when he encounters a huge black bear *(Muin)* coming out of its den. Slowly *Jugwi'ges* backs away so as not to attract any attention towards himself and makes his way back to the village. He knows the bear can be very dangerous this time of year, especially if it is a female who has her cubs nearby. A male bear is very persistent in its attack. When *Jugwi'ges* arrives back at the village he is excited to find the head of the hunter's clan, Robin *(Gopjawej),* at his wigwam to inform him of what he saw. Robin calls for a meeting with the hunters immediately. At this meeting, there are seven hunters, all with names inspired by the birds who demonstrate their special characteristics. Pigeon *(Pules)* is the messenger, Blue Jay *(Ditie's)* is the loud and flashy one, Moose Bird or Grey Jay *(Mikjago'gwetj)* is the one who comes in the last minute, the Owl *(Ku'gu'gwesu)* and a small barn owl *(Gopgwej)* are the night hawks.

Robin instructs the hunters to inform their families that they will be away on expedition, to pack light and to be ready by the break of dawn. The hunt begins with the team following the tracks of the bear along the river. The journey takes them over hills, down valleys, and around lakes and rivers surrounding their territory which spans about a 50-mile radius, and it takes them all summer until late fall before they catch up with the bear.

By this time the bear is heavy, making the deep impressions of its paw tracks much easier to follow. They finally catch up to the bear in a valley surrounded by the Appalachian Mountains common around the northeastern Atlantic region of Turtle Island. Late that evening before they bed down for the night, Robin instructs the crew to get a good rest because the bear is just over the ridge near where they're camped. Robin and Chickadee are the first to go to sleep, but around the campfire that night the rest of the hunters are sipping on tea and talking about the hunt. Blue Jay, who is used to getting a lot of attention because of his beautiful coloured feathers, starts talking about how Robin always gets all the credit, and Pigeon quickly jumps in with his comments because he just likes to gossip and grumble anyway.

Blue Jay points out that they could take the bear down at night because the two owls have night vision and if they travelled fast together, they would be able to catch the bear by surprise. Grey Jay cautions them that it's not a very good idea to go against Robin's "Rules of Order." Blue Jay dismisses his concerns by stating that Grey Jay is just taking sides, because he's scared of the dark. Grey Jay returns, "Robin's family has been in that position for as long as anyone can remember, and his family are born leaders and strategists, so we must obey his orders." *Ditie's* ignores *Mikjago'gwetj* as he summons the other hunters to go with him. *Mikjago'gwetj* does nothing to startle Robin and *Jugwi'ges* in their slumber.

During the night, while the owls are guiding the other hunters to the bear, they get sidetracked by their favourite meals, like rodents and rabbits, which lead them far off track and of course, they all get lost. At daybreak, Robin awakes to find the hunters' camp empty except for *Mikjago'gwetj*, who is still snoring. As Chickadee comes running over and is shocked to see what has happened, Robin gives Grey Jay a nudge and asks him where the others are. Grey Jay, waking up slowly and yawning, explains how the other hunters were envious of Robin and his leadership role. So, to outdo him they decided to go ahead by hunting at night with the two night owls, because they have this "night vision" as Blue Jay says.

Without any comment about the situation, Robin says, "Well, there's still three of us. We should be able to take the bear down if we stick together and follow instructions carefully." They climb up the ridge and look down into the valley where they see the bear foraging around below.

Robin gives careful instructions to the two remaining hunters and says, "From this point on, there's no more talking! We must sneak right up to the bear, to make our attack."

They get about twenty feet from the bear when Robin turns to the hunters to give his final instructions and they realize that *Mikjago'gwetj* is not with them. Robin instructs Chickadee to startle the bear, so he can run in with the spear to pierce him through the heart. This all happens very quickly, and Robin is now shouting with a muffled voice because the bear is now on top of him. He is shouting for Chickadee to get the bear off him by using the part of the spear that has broken off for leverage. As Robin gets out from under the bear, he is soaked with blood, so he wipes it off with his hands and flicks it down as it splatters on the small maple tree saplings nearby.

This blood is like the red on the robin red breast that we commonly see in the spring of the year. In the fall, we will see the red splatters on the maple leaf that mark the bear hunting season and the sky is blood red at sunset. All afternoon they cut portions of the meat for the other hunters that got lost much to Chickadee's dismay. They prepare the heart and the liver for a hunter's meal by gathering some herbs and tubers nearby to make a stew. Chickadee always brings a pot just for this special occasion.

Finally, Chickadee can't stand it anymore, so he asks Robin, "Why do you insist on portioning out the meat for the other hunters when they tried to sabotage the outcome of our expedition and put us at considerable risk and great danger against the bear?" Robin says, "I will explain later. What is more important is that we must finish the work at hand before the sun sets, because other animals will come around when they smell the blood."

By and by, as the stew is just about ready, *Mikjago'gwetj* comes sauntering in to where they are and, smiling from ear to ear, exclaims, "Ahh! Looks like I'm just in time!"

Chickadee jumps up and shouts, "What!"

Just when he's about to attack *Mikjago'gwetj*, Robin cuts him off and turns him around and says to Chickadee, "Whoa! Wait a minute, my little friend. There's something I must tell you. I know you're angry at *Mikjago'gwetj* for what he did, and I don't blame you at all, but remember when you asked me a question a little while ago about why we portioned off the meat for all the other hunters despite what they did? Well, the reason is an important one. You see, we must look at the big picture."

Robin continued, "We must come together. If we start fighting amongst ourselves during the hunt, we will not accomplish our goals, failing not only ourselves, but also our community. When that happens, our community will come apart because we are not working together. One of the most important things my father taught me was to be able to forgive and always stay focused on your goal. We all make mistakes from time to time, but with forgiveness we can always start over to become better people and let go of our failures. I will teach you what he taught me about control. Now go to *Mikjago'gwetj*, and fix him a bowl of our stew."

Chickadee is just beside himself at this request, but Robin nudges him along and says, "Fix him the best of the stew like you would for yourself." Reluctantly Chickadee follows Robin's orders and places the bowl of stew in front of Grey Jay. Geay Jay is delighted with the service that Chickadee gives him, but also very thankful. Finally, the other hunters find their way back to camp, tired but relieved. Robin invites them to join the meal as if nothing happened. The hunters are very grateful for Robin's patience and wisdom and vow to be always loyal to him and from that day forward to maintain the hunter's code of loyalty and respect. So in the fall of the year as the bear is taken down for the hunt, the bear's spirit goes into hibernation, and as it does we can see in the stars that the Big Dipper will be upside down all winter until spring, when the bear will once again come out of its den and renew the cycle of life.

BAD BLOOD

CONSULTING WITH THE SPIRITS WAS first and foremost to determine the nature of what had to be confronted and resolved. One ancient ritual that was practiced by some Wabanaki tribes was bloodletting. This ritual was said to rejuvenate the blood by removing old or bad blood from the system, hence revitalizing the health of the practitioners, and extending their longevity. Sometimes the concept of bad blood could be looked upon as bad relationships, or grudges amongst the people or between tribes. These bad behaviours must also be dealt with as a sickness and removed.

In any case, there were always spiritualists who conducted specific ceremonies that dealt with these matters, people who were highly respected. In most cases, they were the elders or leaders in the community. The elders would first conduct a pipe ceremony and share smoke, then during this ceremony they would have a discussion to determine both the source of—and the solution to—the problem. Following this in the sweat lodge they would consult with the spirits for the best resolution for all. After exiting the lodge, the elders would consult with the leaders of the community and deliver to them their decision, based always on consensus. The leaders then would implement tribal laws to prevent unruly behaviour from spreading. These tribal laws became the traditions, customs, and values that were understood from one tribe to another and that were held and respected within our territories.

For those of us who live in an environment that experiences winter weather that can be extreme at times, we prepare ourselves all throughout the favourable seasons such as spring, summer, and fall. Fall is the season we look towards for that yield of a bountiful crop and processing diverse types of meats. For those who still enjoy the hunt, the wilderness provides a wide variety of animals that are highly sought for their tender meat and nutrition, although in recent years farmers have become the backbone of our nation's food supply. Everywhere on Mother Earth, there are human families co-existing with several types of seasons and climates, and it has been crucial for our survival to know what food source is abundant and sustainable. Over several millennia, we have developed these techniques of adaptation.

The human family continues to develop more and more efficient ways of sustaining the food source by studying the behaviour and reactions of certain life forms in nature, like the changing of the seasons and the effects of the elements under extreme conditions all over the world. As it is told to us in the stars by the Bear and the Seven Hunters, humankind must work together to advance as a team. As a result, we learn to control our environment by inventing means and methods of developing sustainable concepts of farming and processing foods on a monumental scale, all to feed the ever-growing masses of human families on Mother Earth.

NORTH

DIRECTION = NORTH

SEASON = WINTER

SPIRIT GUIDE = POLAR BEAR

ELEMENT = AIR

COLOUR = BLACK

STAGE OF LIFE = SENIOR ELDERS, ANCESTORS, DEATH

MEDICINE= POLYPORE FUNGUS, CHAGA, TOBACCO

ATTRIBUTE = MENTALITY

GIFT = WISDOM/HOPE/FORGIVENESS

THIS IS THE LAST COMPONENT THAT completes the four basic colours of seasons that are commonly used by most or all Native American tribes of North America. They may not all be in the same order of sequence when interpreted, but they are basically the same colours: Black, Red, Yellow, and White.

It was explained to me by an elder who passed away in 1991 named Buffalo Child[4] that some ceremonies don't require the colour black. These teachings were from his spiritual contacts, and one feast ceremony that he conducted required several cotton cloths that were a metre in length and were of all the colours of the rainbow.

A rainbow is our guaranteed symbol of spiritual life after death from our Great Creator. We connect to the spiritual world through our ancestors; they are like our umbilical cords into the spirit world. If we don't maintain our communication with our spiritual guides, we sever those ties and we can become lost. The practice of making offerings to the spirit world is quite common in all cultures of the human family. Always make an offering to your ancestors; they will respond favourably—you'll see. These teachings and many more I learned from Albert Lightning, and I will never forget the statement he always used to make to people who don't believe in spirituality. He used to say, "You have a chance to change things for yourself if you act

[4] Read more about Buffalo Child in "A Song to Awaken the Spirit."

now, when the opportunity presents itself, so do not hesitate, because tomorrow can be too late." The Romans had an equally important saying: *Carpe diem.*

Now as we round the turn and head into the most extreme of all these seasons, we can see a devastating and drastic change come over the environment, especially in northern areas. Freezing weather marches in like an unforgiving military force invading a territory, killing everything in its path. That is kind of a grim perception to have of this season, but that's what happens. All the plants die or freeze into a hibernation state. Every year and everywhere within its reach, the winter season will hold onto the northern regions of Turtle Island with its icy cold grip of snow and frost. In these climates, people must take heed to bundle up with thick furry pelts of animal fur, or whatever they can use to prevent the extreme cold from causing frostbite or even worse, the viral infections that cause us to be immunocompromised in the colder seasons.

Travel is reduced to a crawl because of the icy conditions and more caution is taken when there is a snowstorm, especially if it's a blizzard. Yes, Old Man Winter takes his toll when one does not respect his extreme season. Often, those who ignore the extreme conditions and don't prepare properly, will pay the ultimate price of death. Winter is a very dark season; the days are noticeably short, but the nights, of course, are long. These are some of the logical reasons why the colour black is associated with this direction. Our ancestors, however, found ways to use these testing times to their advantage. One important ceremony conducted by elders during these long, cold winter nights was the establishing and reaffirmation of the clan systems within the Grand Council, a mid-winter feast ceremony.

Since time immemorial, the Mi'kmaw people have practiced sacred ceremonies that maintain the knowledge of our bloodlines. It was a way of making sure that people didn't marry too close to their relatives, because to do so would create bad blood and could cause deformities and other types of birth defects. The head chief in each district would call this meeting and hear from his subordinate chiefs of plans for weddings, funerals, or expansion of hunting territories within the district. This would all take place inside a large longhouse built of birch bark. As women and children were not allowed in these meetings, it was predominately men, except for a couple of elder clan mothers. This get-together would last about a week and would involve hours of storytelling, songs, and dances. Smudging and smoking of the pipe was a customary practice during these conferences, especially sharing of medicines both herbal and spiritual, so it would involve elaborate ceremonies with prayers using a mixture of sweet grass, sages, cedar and the fungus off the white birch tree that we call *jigoqs*.

In Siberia, some people call this fungus *chaga,* and in other areas they also used this medicine to strengthen the immune system and help prevent colds and flus. Much respect was given to the wise elders who had long memories or those that could remember the old ways. Mi'kmaq people say *sibida'sit:* the ability to remember ancient times, or to stretch the memory. *Jigoqs* would cleanse the mind of negative thinking and help to focus on the truth and the reality during confusing times when there are too many things going on in a person's mind. These are times when your thoughts are clouded, and decisions can become difficult to make. When it is applied as a medicine, it's combined with meditation and prayer to give it its full strength, and is very effective for people with who may struggle with fever, or other conditions.

THE POLAR BEAR

ALTHOUGH THERE ARE SOME VERY unusual and interesting creatures that can live under extreme conditions of hot and cold upon our Mother Earth, one of the most notable, that has become an icon for this vast northern region, is the polar bear. *Muin Wapskw* is what we call him in Mi'kmaq, along with several other creatures of the north that have adapted to the extreme wintry conditions through millennia and have made it their home. The polar bear is our animal spirit guide of the north and teaches us to focus, concentrate, and always keep our wits about us, especially when travelling during the winter storms. By observing how the polar bear hunts and survives, we gain his knowledge and strength. In fact, that's how the polar bear has come to rely on the cycle and the ebb and flow of what the tides bring with each changing season.

Our brothers of the far north, a nation of people called the Inuit, have decided to live in these harsh barren lands, and have adjusted to the climate and what it provides for their survival. The Inuit share with us their fantastic stories and experiences that sometimes border on the extraordinary.

Of all the animals within their range in this vast remote northern region, it is *Nanuk* the polar bear that is considered to be the spirit guide and the symbol of the far north. Inuit hunters consider *Nanuk* to be wise, powerful, and almost a man. Some call the polar bear "the great lonely roamer." In the past, the Inuit ate polar bear meat and used the fur to make warm trousers for men and *kamiks* (soft boots) for women. An average polar bear yielded three pairs of trousers and one *kamik.* The liver was the only part of the bear that was never eaten. It could make even sled dogs violently ill. Hunters paid respect to *Nanuk's* soul, *Tatkok,* by hanging the skin in an honoured place in his igloo for several days. If the bear had been male, the hunter offered its spirit tools such as knives and bow-drills; if female, the hunter offered knives, skin-scrapers, and needle cases. There are many, many stories and legends about the great polar bear and the Inuit, but this one helps explain why he was considered part man:

> Once there was a poor hunter. He always went out but never got anything. Finally, one day he saw a polar bear. As he crawled toward it over the ice, the bear said to him, "Don't shoot me. If you follow me and do what I say, I will make it so you will always be able to get whatever animals you think about." The bear told the man to climb on his back and close his eyes. "Do not open them until I tell you to." Then, the man and the bear went down into the sea a long way. "Do not open your eyes," the bear reminded him. Finally, they came back up and the man saw an igloo along the edge of the pack ice. They went inside, and the man saw another bear with a spear in his haunch. The first bear said, "If you can take that spear out of the bear and make him well, you will become a good hunter."
>
> The man broke off the shaft, eased the spear point out of the bear's haunch, and the wound began to heal. Then the first bear took off his bearskin "parka" and became a man. After the wound was

healed completely, the bear-man put back on his bearskin "parka," told the poor hunter to climb on his back and close his eyes, and together they went back into the sea. When the bear finally stopped, he asked the man to open his eyes. Looking around, the man realized he had been returned to the spot from which he began his journey. He thought he had only been gone a day, but on arriving home he found that he had been away a month. From then on, the man was always a good hunter.[5]

[5] Source: https://en.wikipedia.org/wiki/Nanook

FULL CIRCLE

SO, THIS BRINGS US FULL CIRCLE with the hunt to understand what life is all about. Right from the very beginning, we must track where we've come from, and where we are going. How far time will take us into the future we can only predict with our scientific technology and our imaginations. But we will never truly know, and some things will always remain a mystery and should never be known. My favourite saying is "No one person can ever know it all."

Only the Great Creator knows these things and we as a human family should respect that. Discover new knowledge when it presents itself, learn through experience, share and enjoy a beautiful life as it unfolds for you, and always believe in a higher power regardless of what that may be. It will give you strength to endure the most demanding situations that you may have to confront in life.

For sacred thought, the time is right now because of the chaos in the modern world we live in. We need some good, wholesome Indigenous medicine and spiritual values that can lead us towards peace and harmony with all humankind.

Life is truly a gift. Don't abuse it.

A SONG TO AWAKEN THE SPIRIT: MY JOURNEY TO THE MI'KMAQ HONOUR SONG

THIS IS A STORY ABOUT MY JOURNEY into the revival of the traditional spiritual movement that began here among the Mi'kmaq in the mid-seventies. The help and teachings of many elders along the way would guide me to understand how to apply good medicine for my people and everyone.

As a young Mi'kmaq boy, I grew up on the Indian reservation called Red Bank in the Province of New Brunswick, Canada. In my younger days between the ages of four to eight years old, I enjoyed playing outdoors with my friends that lived nearby. My favourite daily activity was going down the river with my makeshift fishing rod, made of an alder branch stick that my father gave me, some string, and a bait hook or a safety pin when I couldn't find a real hook. Some of my friends would join me at times and bring breadcrumbs to throw in the water. We all sat on a huge rock at low tide fishing for minnows and chubs that would chase the breadcrumbs in a little pool behind the rock.

The summer days seemed to be so long in my younger days, and full of adventure. We used to play in the puddles after the rains and always played on the ground with the insects. We captured many frogs and set horseflies free with a string of ants on their tails. They would never get very far because there was always a bird nearby to fetch them right out of the air and we would roll over laughing.

Living on the reservation in the 1950s and 60s was a difficult time for most people. There was not much employment, and everyone was poor, but we all shared everything as much as possible, especially food. It seemed like every family was big, and some children would stay with smaller families to help with chores.

But times were changing fast and in the early 60s, a lot of Indian children became the target of the Sixties Scoop, meaning they were picked up and taken to Indian Residential Schools far, far away. There was a lot of drinking back in those days, and our parents fought a lot and would separate. My two older sisters and I wound up staying at our next-door neighbour's, and one day a big car drove into the driveway.

A tall white man came into the house, introduced himself as the Sheriff, and said to the man and woman that were taking care of us that he was going to be taking charge of the children now.

For a young Mi'kmaq Indian boy just barely eight years old, this was a whole other world of experience for me, and it was traumatizing, to say the least. Although I cried and tried to run away, down the river to hide behind some bushes, the adults were much stronger. They found me, picked me up, and forced me and my two older sisters to go with the white man in his car. I was broken-hearted as I looked out the window of that car, watching my familiar neighbourhood disappear behind my tears. I don't recall how long it took but finally, I must have cried myself to sleep. Somewhere along the way, we stopped just off the road to have lunch by a picnic table. I was still so upset that I did not want to eat, so the man tried to force me to eat a sandwich. I fought back and started running towards the road.

I was running across the road when I heard my sisters crying out, "George, don't run away, please come back!" I stopped at the edge of the road just as a transport truck was zooming by, and the wind from the speed of the truck pushed me down into the gravel ditch. As I got to my feet, the tall man grabbed me and beat me, telling me to never do that again. He took me back and locked me in the car, kicking and screaming. My sisters begged me to stay with them and not run away.

When I arrived at the Indian Residential School in Shubenacadie, Nova Scotia, with my two older sisters, we stood in front at the main entrance way into the school, which was in the middle of the huge brick-like building that looked like a castle. There were girls on one side of the building and boys on the opposite end, but this time they were allowed to gather closer to where we seemed to be on display. It was hard for me to understand what they were all talking about because back home we only spoke mostly in the Mi'kmaq language.

All the boys there were shouting, "New guy! New guy!" and hearing that, I started looking around to see what was on fire, because in our Mi'kmaq language *Nu'kai* means "I'm on fire!" which sounds the same as what they were saying. But was I on fire?

Suddenly a fight broke out right in front of us between two boys that were about my age. They were quickly separated and ushered away by the supervisors. Later, I found out that they were fighting over who was going to be my best friend.

This I found to be strange. The kids established a kind of pecking order like wolves would do in a pack. There were big guys and little guys, and the big guys would protect the little guys, but the little guys had to pay the big guys for their cake or their orange on Sundays, which was the only time it was served as a dessert. The trick was to be able to sneak it out of the refectory without getting caught. The nuns were always patrolling back and forth while everyone ate.

Every child that arrived there went through the same little ritual, their ages ranging from six to sixteen. We were assigned a number that would be sewn on all our clothes and marked on our lockers, beds, and shoes, to keep track of our belongings, especially on laundry day. It was regimental, almost like a military—and highly disciplinary.

The supervisors were not Indian, nor were the nuns or the brothers running the school.

There were many rules at the school, and the administration used a leather strap to punish the Indian boys and girls if we broke any rules. These strappings were severe beatings on the hands, but sometimes stretched up the tender part of the arm almost to the elbow. If you pulled your hand away before you got strapped and the supervisor missed, another strike would be added to your list of demerits.

One of the rules was never to speak our Mi'kmaq language, which was the hardest thing for me to do because I spoke almost no English, or at least I didn't speak it very well.

Everyone had chores to do, attended school for most of the day, and did not have much playtime. In the evening, we got on our knees to say the rosaries. It seemed there were prayers for everything, but especially on Sundays. Prayers were said when we lined up for breakfast, prayers were said during breakfast, after breakfast, when we lined up for school, during the school day, rosaries in the evening, night prayers before bed, and morning prayers at bedside.

There were a lot of fights and disputes among the boys throughout the school year, sometimes brought on by the supervisors, who favoured certain individuals over others. This caused a lot of jealousy. Most of the time, it was because of debts owed for protection from schoolyard bullies.

Sometimes, to break the tension, the supervisors would come out with a huge bucket of marbles, all different sizes, and have everyone come outside near the baseball field. "Scramble!" they would call out, throwing the marbles randomly as far as they could into the field. Everybody in turn would run out, grabbing handfuls of the marbles.

It was like feeding time for the chickens on the farm, and

we all ran to grab as many marbles as we could. Whoever grabbed the most won a prize. Then there would be an outdoor tournament where a little hole was made in the ground and two boys would compete, trying to get the most marbles in the hole.

There were times we had fun, but there were sad times, too. We all felt the pain when somebody accidentally broke an arm or a leg, but the worst pain was when somebody was sexually abused by the supervisors. The nuns, the brothers, and even the priests all seemed to be involved, but they made sure the abuse was covered up, and nobody was to speak a word of it or they would be punished.

Some of the boys and girls would go home in summer and return to school at the end of August, but there were a few that stayed all year round. As I grew accustomed to the Residential School after being there for a few years, I eventually spoke English very well.

The Shubenacadie Indian Residential School was closed in 1967, the centennial year of the union of Canada and its one hundred years of formation.

By now I was a teen going to high school in Sunny Corner across the river from my community. I would eventually go on to finish school and start travelling. In my travels, I met a lot of new friends that invited me to join in following the Traditional Revival Movement that was evolved from the hippie movement of the early sixties, accompanied by the feel-good music of the rock and roll era.

At the time, a small group in New Brunswick asked me to join them in gatherings from time to time. They were dedicated to following the spiritual teachings of medicine men and women from many Indian nations of North America.

One of my journeys was to attend an ecumenical conference hosted in Morley, Alberta, by Chief John Snow around 1980. As a young man now, I was eager to go on my own and challenge the world. What I saw and experienced there had a huge impact. There were spiritual leaders and medicine men from all around the world. Some of these elders spoke of prophecies that were to unfold in the present times, and said that the native youth at the time may be part of what was to be revealed.

One of these elders and spiritual leaders was Albert Lightning and he would play a very important role in our traditional spiritual revival here on the East Coast with the Mi'kmaq. His first visit was in the mid-seventies in Shubenacadie, Nova Scotia. He would return to the Atlantic region, including New Brunswick and Prince Edward Island, several times over the next sixteen years.

In 1981, I organized the first powwow in my own community of Metepenagiag (Red Bank) and invited Buffalo Child (also known as Albert Lightning) to attend. There, he conducted his sacred ceremonies and spoke of his prophecies to all that attended in his 30-foot tipi.

He also spoke of another gathering that would call for all Indigenous people to come together and express their traditional customs and values to the world, and called for it to take place the following summer of 1982, in Regina, Saskatchewan.

So that summer I took a train with a friend of mine to travel out there. At this conference, there was a designated elders' camp set up in the flatlands of the plains outside of Regina. Thousands of Indigenous peoples from around the world gathered there. Tipis had been put up by their owners who travelled there from across the continent of North America. It was like walking into a dream of an ancient village, to see so many brown-skinned Native peoples from all tribes, standing strong their braids and a real "traditional" look.

You could hear drumming and chanting all day and night. It was truly a magical experience, just to be there. They had also set up a powwow dancing area that was almost half a mile long because there were so many people there. When they had the grand entry dance, there were almost 2,000 dancers in the lineup and about 50 drum groups that took turns doing a grand entry dance song, one right after another until the dancers made a complete circle. Tears rolled down my face, as I had never seen or witnessed such power and dignity from the humblest nations of the world.

By this time, I was attending a lot of ceremonies and becoming more experienced in the traditional ceremonial ways of the ancient ones. With the teachings of the spiritual leader from Hobbema, Alberta, I forged a path to communicate with the spirits through fasting. My first experience was to fast near an ancient burial mound across the river from my community, now known as the Augustine Mound. It was during this fast that I started to get some direction from my ancestors. I experienced a vision there that told me to travel out west where I would meet more elders who could teach me more.

In 1983, Buffalo Child invited me and a few followers to attend a Sun Dance ceremony put on by Harold Cardinal and his family, who resided 40 miles north of Edmonton, Alberta, near the community called Alexander—a Cree Reservation.

Buffalo Child introduced us as his followers from the East Coast to the Cardinal family, and asked if we could participate in their Sun Dance ceremony, which they readily accepted. Once the huge 8-foot high, 25-foot diameter circular lodge was constructed, everyone participated

Every man, woman, and child helped in some way to build the structure, which took all day to complete. I was given the task of helping some elders prepare tobacco ties and what they called *prints.* These were offerings made of cloth about a metre long and each one was a different colour.

The elders said the all colours of the rainbow were to be included, and that this represented hope, and the vision and dream that these spiritual ceremonies would help change the world, with peace and understanding for all of humankind. These would be hung inside the ceiling of the Sun Dance Lodge as offerings for the ancestors.

This Sun Dance was not like the usual Plains Sioux Sun Dances of the Lakota, which required the piercing through the chest or the dragging of a buffalo skull as a form of sacrifice as spiritual medicine. These sacrifices were meant to offer their pain and suffering to the spirits, and to bring about the healing that the people needed.

At this Sun Dance, all ages and groups of men, women, and children were allowed to participate, if they were fasting, which meant no food or water. Inside the lodge hung a wild and loose rainbow, hung from the ceiling as cloth offerings about a metre long, which danced and dangled down with tobacco ties on the ends of them.

The lodge was divided into two groups, males on one side and females on the other. There was a willow fence about 4 feet high which all the dancers stood behind and about 4 feet away from the wall facing the centre pole. The door—8 feet high by 10 feet wide—was where outsiders could watch and sometimes test the dancers to see if they might break under criticism and laughter.

Inside the lodge was a group of elders that sat on the ground playing on their hand drums and singing ceremonial songs. All the dancers were given an eagle bone whistle, a band of braided sage to wear as a crown, and wristbands of buffalo sage.

There was a man with a stick in the centre, who instructed everyone to focus on a line that he had marked on the centre pole. He was very strict and walked all around the circle making sure nobody was cheating. He instructed the dancers to blow on the eagle whistle in unison with a steady rhythm and to bounce on the balls of their feet together all the while keeping rhythm with two eagle plume feathers in each hand. We danced all day until the sun went down but stayed in the lodge all night.

The next day at first light everyone was woken up by an elder who was chanting all around the ceremonial grounds, almost like calling everyone to wake up and pray. The dancers were ordered to prepare and dance all day. The instructor again went through the rules and said that if anyone wanted to leave, they could at any time, but they could not come back. Some adults and most of the children left but were taken care of by the Sun Dance helpers once they went out, and were given a special feast ceremony to end their fast.

Throughout the day as the ceremony continued an unusual event took place: I experienced a vision. My eyes shifted like a shutter speed in a camera, and I saw thousands of Native people all in regalia dancing over a hill of grass.

At first, I could see only their heads and shoulders. But when it happened again, I went down behind and started rubbing my eyes. The instructor came and hit me with the stick and told me to get up or get out. The second time I went down I could see more of the dancers from head to toe. Beautiful regalia of all the tribes from North America and in the front leading the dance I could see dancers with Mi'kmaq designs on their regalia. They were all singing this song and chanting like a choir, and everyone was singing it.

During one of the breaks, the elders asked if somebody had a vision of a song, but I was too shy and didn't want to reveal what I had seen. I thought it was part of the ceremony and that someone else was going to sing. But no one spoke up and the ceremony continued. I wondered about that for some time after. *Had I been meant to speak up about my experience?*

When Sun Dance was over, everyone that participated in the lodge took part in a sacred feast ceremony. The group from the East Coast followed Albert Lightning to his home in Hobbema, Alberta. After a few days of visiting, we went on another journey to the sacred grounds in Kootenay Plains. There were many people from different parts of the world

that would attend the sacred ceremonies of the Indigenous people of North America at this site.

There were remnants of sacred lodges everywhere, some of which had been there for many years and were weather-beaten. There were sweat lodges, Sun Dance lodges, and shaking tent lodges. These were places where people went to fast and seek vision quests. This was the perfect place to fast, the beautiful mountains all around feeding the turquoise-coloured mountain water, into rivers, into creeks.

But it was a little dangerous as well, because in this area roamed grizzly bears, mountain lions, and wolves. The beauty of nature was so overwhelming, it was easy to forget the risk of danger nearby, until you heard one of them.

After setting up camp the East Coast group gathered around the campfire at night and talked about if anyone else was going to go through a fast again. I was so anxious, I said I would, and made a commitment to do so the very next day.

I didn't have the materials to put up a lodge, so I asked the elder what I should do. The elder told me that I still could fast without a lodge, but it would be more difficult and testing. If I stayed near the camp, he thought it would be safer. I wandered around our camp for a couple of days, until the third day, when I decided to climb up the mountain and sit on the ledge. I sat there all day meditating and thinking about how I could help my people get back to the traditional ceremonial ways.

After conducting a pipe ceremony, I made my way back down the mountain, still thinking about what I might be able to do when I got back home. When I got to the bottom, I thought about how beautiful it was for the people out there to still have their ceremonies, songs, dances, and especially their language.

I asked myself, What did my people do to lose such a beautiful culture? Did my people sell out? Did they give up? Were they ashamed of our traditional way of life? Suddenly I was overwhelmed with sadness, and I realized that I had no answer to these daunting questions. I thought about watching the children playing at the powwow grounds, who laughed and spoke their own language, and it brought me back to a time when I used to play as a young boy and speak in my own language, too. I felt so sad I started crying. I cried louder and louder, and it seemed I couldn't stop, I was just letting it all flow from my heart. It was like I had a broken heart that my people had let us down.

As the day ended, I went back to camp and informed the elder that I would be finished the following day. The elder said that there would be a sweat lodge for all of us to attend in the afternoon. It was here when the elder asked me to sing the song. I didn't realize then that I had received a song, so the elder told me it will come to you when you're ready. Everyone was preparing for the sacred feast ceremony that night, which would be inside a huge 30-foot-tall tipi belonging to Albert Lightning.

I was waiting beside the community fire when I heard this beautiful chanting coming from somewhere nearby. As I scanned the camping area, I noticed a sweat lodge in progress a short distance away. The chanting was kind of haunting and it intrigued me. I went over to investigate. When I got there, the doorman was a white man that had been assisting Albert Lightning for many years as a helper. I asked if I could join, and he said he would ask the elder when the door opened.

When the door opened, out crawled three old white men with beards. I was surprised because I distinctly heard chanting that sounded like a group of Indigenous men chanting in the Cree language. I asked the doorkeeper what was going on.

He said that these men were priests that were sent here by the Pope to investigate the spiritual practices of Indigenous people and that they were from different denominations of the Catholic faith. I asked if there was anyone else inside the lodge that was Native and he said no, just the elder. Then I asked him who was chanting in the lodge. He said these priests learned the chant in the sweat lodge and they had never heard it before.

After everyone had finished their sweat lodge ceremonies, we all headed to the large ceremonial tipi. After everyone was seated, Albert Lightning began with a pipe ceremony, then the feast was served. During the ceremony, the priests wanted to share their experiences with the Indigenous ceremonies and why they were sent by the Pope.

Each one of them spoke praise for the Indigenous ceremonies. They all expressed that it was a beautiful experience. One of them took the time to explain in detail, and these are his words. "If God wanted human beings to pray and worship him—" He paused, with a tear in his eye, then he said, "This is what I believe he would prefer." He went on to explain that it was the humblest experience that they had ever participated in. He said that our Indigenous prayers included everything in creation, praying for everyone else first and leaving yourself until last, which was a true expression of humility.

Kootenay Plains, Alberta, is a sacred space and I believe miracles have been born there for many Indigenous people, who have changed their own lives for the better and have brought about healing and wellness for everyone, including people who are not Indigenous.

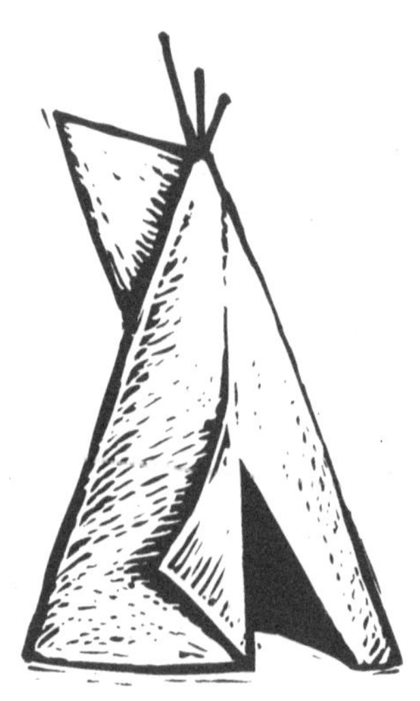

The following year, in 1984, a blind man from Shubenacadie went to attend a sweat lodge ceremony on the eel grounds. He was very interested in learning about the traditional ceremonies and wanted us to teach him.

During the sweat lodge, he saw something in me and made a proclamation that I was to sing a song for the people. This reminded me of what the elder had told me the year before: "It will come to you when you're ready," he said. The time was now and it was clear. I knew what my people needed, and they needed it immediately.

They needed the message in this song, which was to honour and respect one another—to build on their culture, to identify, and to be proud of who they are. The words came instinctively. I sang the song every opportunity I had, at powwows and even funerals. I helped start many drum groups and helped organize many powwows with my newfound traditional family in Atlantic Canada.

From 1988 to 1991, I worked as a director of a federally funded halfway house pilot project for Indigenous men in Charlottetown, PEI, that hosted many Mi'kmaq men, some who were homeless, and others who were coming out of incarceration.

My job was to teach traditional knowledge including ceremonies such as the sweat lodge, drumming, dancing, herbal medicines, and craft making. Before I left, the President of the Native Council of PEI at the time, Graham Tuplin, asked me to do a recording of all the Mi'kmaq songs that I had been teaching the people for the past four years there.

In this recording were five of my own original songs which I wrote including "The Mi'kmaq Honour Song," "Gathering Song," "Canoe Song," "Spring Thunders," and "The Dance of Vigour." The first professional recordings were made on cassette tapes and titled *Traditional Mi'kmaq Chants by George Paul.* Now they are on the Internet and have been shared around the world, thanks to Facebook, YouTube, and other multimedia venues.

This young man that grew up to be an elder with humble beginnings still shares the story of the one song that the spirits gave to him on that day, in the Kootenay Plains, so many years ago. A song that would awaken in him the Mi'kmaq spirit, "The Mi'kmaq Honour Song" has brought healing to many people and continues to build unity for all people.

I have heard many testimonies from people I met along the way that explained to me that the song was so inspiring it changed their lives to be a much better person and it influenced them to tell others to do the same.

THE HONOUR SONG

Let us honour the people we are.
My People, let us unite!
Let us honour our ancestral lineage.

My people, let us help one another.
Let us help one another the way
Our Creator has placed us here upon
Mother Earth.

Way oh hay hi ya
Ya way yo hay yo hay hi ya
Way yo hay hi ya
Ya way yo hay hi ya
Way yo hay hi ya
Way yo hay hi ya
Ya way yo hay ha ya hay yo

GLOSSARY

MI'KMAQ TRANSLATIONS DIFFER FROM area to area, and we are thankful to Francis-Smith orthography of Nova Scotia and Eunice Metallic of Listuguj for being the keepers of our Mi'kmaq languages. The words I share today are known all around Wabanaki, although some may be specific to our area of Atlantic Canada.

Buktew: Fire

Buoins: Dreamers

E'pit: Woman

Ekjibuktew: Sacred fire

Gaqtugwaq: Thunder Beings

Gaqtugwaw Sisip (or Gulu): Thunder Bird

Ginaps: Leaders

Gisu'lk Ikji-niskam: Great Grandfather Creator

Gitpu: Eagle spirit

Gopgwej: Small barn owl

Gopjawej: Robin

Inuit: Most northern nation

Jigoqs: Fungus

Jugwi'ges: Chickadee, one of the seven Mi'kmaq hunters

Kamiks: Soft boots for women

Ku'gu'gwesu: Owl

Maqamigew: Earth

Mestugepegajit: Buffalo

Mikjago'gwetj: Moose bird or grey jay

Muin Wapskw: Polar bear

Muin: Black bear

Musigisk: Father Sky

N'nu'g (or Ilnu'g): The human people

Na Tliaj: It will be

Na'gweg: Day

Nanuk: Polar bear (not a Mi'kmaq word)
Netugulite'wk: The Story of the Seven Hunters
Niskaminu Na'gu'set: Sun Spirit
Niskaminu: Grandfather Sun
Nugumi: Grandmother Moon
Pegenuk: Darkest night
Pepgwejeda'q: The first drum
Pules: Pigeon
Sabe'wig Guto'qa'taqan: Sacred Wheel
Samqwan: Water
Sibida'sit: To stretch the memory
Tahoe!: A victory shout that translates loosely as "Right on!"
Tatkok: Nanuk the polar bear's soul (not a Mi'kmaq word)
Tepgunaset: Moon
Titie's: Blue jay
Ukju'sn: Air
Uksitqamu: Mother / planet earth
Wa'ji'j: Mi'maq marker poles with clan symbols on them
Wa'so'q: The heavens

IMAGE CREDITS

The artworks on pages 16, 42, 44, 48, 66, and 115 are by George Paul and appear courtesy of the artist.

The images on pages 21, 31, 34–35, and 51 were submitted by the author.

The images on pages 25, 38, 54, 57, 59, 64, 71, 82, 87, 105, and 109 are sourced from Shutterstock.com.

The book cover reproduced on page 93, copyright author George Paul and illustrator Loretta Gould, appears with the permission of the publisher, Éditions Bouton d'or Acadie.

ABOUT THE AUTHOR

ELDER GEORGE PAUL, Spirit name "Sky Blue Eagle," was born on Metepenagiag First Nation, which runs along the Miramichi River in New Brunswick. For over four decades, he has been involved with the Indigenous Traditional Movement to support the revival of Mi'kmaq songs, chants, and ceremonies. A leader in the field of Indigenous Studies, Elder Paul is the author of two previous books, *Le chant d'honneur · The Honour Song · Kepmite'taqney Ktapekiaqn* (Éditions Bouton d'or Acadie) and *My Journey to The Honour Song*. He has also been involved in the production of several documentaries with the University of New Brunswick, Aboriginal Peoples Television Network (APTN), and the CBC.